AYURVEDA

The Complete Programme
for your Well-being

Important Notice:

This book was carefully prepared, according to the most recent information.
Nevertheless, all information is supplied without liability.
The publisher can accept no responsibility for potential detriment and injury,
which result from following the practical advice in this book.
The pieces of advice contained in this book do not replace the examination and care given by a doctor.
Before carrying out a treatment on yourself, you should consult a doctor, especially if you suffer
from a health complaint, take regular medication or are pregnant.

List of picture sources:

Corel, Ontario/ce: 29 top
creativ collection, Freiburg/Breisgau: miniatures 10–24, 29–32
Maharishi Ayur-Veda Centre, Bad Ems: 1, 34 bottom, 36, miniatures 33–36
MEV, Augsburg: 5, 12 middle. 25, 32 left., 33, miniatures 4–9, 61–64
Parkschlößchen Bad Wildstein, Traben-Trarbach: 2, 41, miniatures 50–60
PhotoPress, Stockdorf/Munich: 6, 7, 8, 9, 10, 11, 12 top, 12 bottom,
13, 14, 15, 16, 17, 22, 23, 24, 26, 28, 29 bottom, 30, 31, 32 right, 34 top, 42, 52
VEMAG, Cologne: 4, 37, 38, 39, 40, 50, 51, 53, 54, 55, 56, 57, 58, 59, 60, miniatures 25–28, 37–41
Michael Wollert: 43, 44, 45, 46, 47, 48, 49, miniatures 42–49

Ayurveda

© Neuer Pawlak Verlag
Part of the VEMAG Verlags- und Medien Aktiengesellschaft, Cologne
Author: Georgia Schwarz
Cover: Jump, Hamburg
Produced by: Neuer Pawlak Verlag, Cologne

ISBN 3-86146-028-9

CONTENTS

FOREWORD

Ayurveda, the complete natural medicine and teachings on nutrition, also shows you how to achieve beauty and lead an active life.

In recent years the triumphal march of Ayurveda has been unstoppable, also in the West. More and more people are choosing the integral way to relaxation and healing and live according to the basic rules of Ayurveda, which is the oldest medical teaching known to us, according to different researchers. As an integral healing method, Ayurveda concentrates on precaution and the maintaining of health – not on the treatment of illnesses. In this book we would like to introduce you to a form of Ayurveda, which is modern and has been adapted to the West: Maharishi-Ayurveda, named after the Indian scholar, Maharishi Mahesh Yogi. On no account can our advice replace an Ayurvedic health treatment with spe-

cialised diagnoses and individually adapted therapeutic measures or the treatment of severe health complaints by a doctor or an Ayurvedic therapist. We would rather familiarise you with the basis of Ayurveda and the way of life shown in the Ayurvedic teachings. Apart from that, we will introduce you to the applications and techniques, which you can easily copy at home and which will help you to achieve inner peace and balance on a daily basis.

If you are interested in a comprehensive Ayurveda treatment, then consult your local Yellow Pages or the internet.

WHAT IS AYURVEDA?

The term "Ayurveda" is a word from the Sanskrit, the old Indian standard and invented language. It is put together from the roots *"ayus"*, meaning *life* and *"vit"*, meaning *knowledge*. The focal point of Ayurveda rests in the preservation and restoration of full health for body, mind and soul, which form one unit in this Indian healing method. According to the teachings of Ayurveda, full health can only be reached then when a balance exists between all levels; that means body, mind and soul.

Ayurvedic medicine is about an extensive health system, which is defined less through the treatment of specific illnesses than being based on dealing with body and mind through a definite perception of life.

This special dealing consists of the following components:

- Detoxification (panchakarma)
- The right nutrition
- Yoga exercises
- Applications using herbs and massage techniques
- Meditation and prayer

THE HUMAN BEING – A MICROCOSM IN A MACROCOSM

Ayurveda is not only concerned with health but also with the relationship of the human being with something greater, with the cosmos. According to the teachings of Ayurveda, our personal welfare is inseparable, along with health, from nature and the environment.

The human being represents, so to speak, a microcosm and a macrocosm. He is a small, but complete reflection of the great cosmic picture. Therefore everything, which effects the human being, also influences the macrocosm.

Ayurveda makes the assumption that each creation, and therefore also each human being, is an individual expression of inner consciousness and is integrated into the unity of nature and the cosmos. If this unity is broken up and the self is lost, illnesses develop, problems occur. This is caused by a "fault of the intellect", as it is called in Ayurveda prakyaparab. Such faults can be avoided when one makes decisions that are based on the unity of the self. So that you are aware of your inner self, you should try not to take too much notice of outside influences.

THE ORIGIN AND HISTORY OF AYURVEDA

Ayurveda is an eastern healing method with a tradition going back thousands of years. Nowadays it is practised mainly in India and Sri Lanka. Many researchers think that Ayurveda represents the oldest medical teaching known to us – it is older than Chinese medicine and much older than our western medicine. Due to this ancient tradition and the diverse contents, one suspects that Ayurveda is the origin of all medical teaching.

THE VEDA

The first writing about Ayurveda can be found in the Veda. They are regarded as not only the oldest pieces of evidence of Indian culture and medicine but also as by far the oldest writings by mankind handed down to us. These Veda, written in Sanskrit, contain the entire knowledge about Ayurveda. The Veda consists of four manuscripts: the Rig-Veda is the oldest text with a total of 1028 hymns. Descriptions

of operations, prostheses and the effects of over 50 medicinal plants can already be found. Then follow the Yajur-Veda and the Sama-Veda, which were written 3000 years before Christ.

The Atharva-Veda, which was written down about 1200 years before Christ, is the most important source for Ayurveda. Here you can already find over 300 medicinal plants and many types of therapy for most diverse ailments.

According to Indian philosophy, Rig-Veda had already been revealed by the gods thousands of years before it was written down. Therefore the Veda are regarded as being timeless and represent the "structures of our consciousness, brought about by sound and shape".

FROM THEN UNTIL NOW

The high point of the Ayurvedic healing art occurs between 200 and 500 years before Christ. The methods of therapy described by Indian healers then are still definitive for Ayurvedic diagnoses and therapy today. Since this time, the "science of healthy life" has become an essential part of teaching at Indian universities.

During the following centuries Ayurveda fell again into oblivion. Above all, when India belonged to the British monarchy, from 1839 until 1947, did the western system of values influence Indian philosophy. Only at the time of the Indian independence movement under Mahatma Ghandi did one remember again the old healing methods in India. Nowadays there exists in India a strong link between Ayurveda and the

traditional social, intellectual and cultural structures. Here, the concept of the body, mind and soul is just beginning to gain significance. After all, the strict separation of body and mind played an important role in western medicine for a long time.

THE MAHARISHI-AYURVEDA

The most widely practised form of Ayurveda in the West today is that of the Indian scholar, Maharishi Mahesh Yogi, the Guru of the Beatles and many other prominent figures. Under his leadership at the beginning of the seventies Ayurvedic doctors and scribes translated the original Ayurveda texts into the Indian language used today. Western scientists transferred these into the so-called Maharishi-Ayurveda for the prevailing living conditions in the West.

AYURVEDA AS A THERAPY

The highest aim of Ayurveda is to achieve a long life without disease and without sorrow, as well as to tap intellectual potential through the development of consciousness and spiritual far-sightedness. Ayurveda is not aimed primarily at healing disease; rather its aim is to hold these at bay through a healthy way of life and intellectual occupation.

The primary goal of the Ayurveda practised in Europe and in the USA is to correct the existing pattern of our thoughts, feelings and behaviour and to bring the human being into line with himself – which

according to Maharishi-Ayurveda is the ordering and healing place in a person.

THE TERM "HEALTH" IN AYURVEDA

The Ayurvedic term for health – swastha – means, "to be proven in the self". Roughly paraphrased, health in Ayurveda means order. Disease, on the other hand, means disorder. Order and disorder exist in our bodies in a state of constant interaction. According to Ayurveda, one becomes healthy by being aware of the disorder in one's body and trying to re-establish order.

All physical and spiritual-intellectual functions are controlled by the three basic strengths, the so-called doshas, Vata, Pitta and Kapha (see page 11 ff.). If an equal balance exists between these three strengths then we are healthy.

The eight therapeutic disciplines in Ayurveda

In Ayurveda there are eight therapeutic disciplines, which can be extended on every level. They contain detailed methods of treatment for the following areas:

- *Surgery*
- *Medication*
- *Gynaecology*
- *Paediatric medicine*
- *Intoxification*
- *Treatment of ear, nose and throat illnesses*
- *Rejuvenation*
- *Invigoration*

What does balance mean?

In order to understand Ayurveda it is important to define the term "balance". Balance does not mean that all components have to be available in the same measures. It is concerned much more with achieving an individual balance, which corresponds with each personality.

In Ayurveda there are three known causes that can lead to a disturbance of balance between the three energies of life; Vata, Pitta and Kapha.

- Our sense organs become overstrained, for example through noise, a hectic pace of life, poor nutrition, too little peace and time to recover, or you lack any stimulation – you go about in a daze.

- We use our senses and spirit in the wrong way – for example, we torment ourselves with negative thoughts because of high expectations and we ignore our body's signals.

- We neglect the influence of time (daily, nightly or seasonal rhythm), of our age and of our diet.

A disturbance of balance of the three doshas has a negative effect on the organism. If you undertake suitable counter-measures, for example regular rest and relaxation and change your diet and life style, your organism will be successful in re-establishing balance between the three doshas through self-healing powers available. If, however, this imbalance has existed for a long time, the self-healing powers of the body will not be enough: one will become ill.

THE SIX LEVELS OF UNBALANCE (KRIYAKALA)

In the case of an unbalance that has existed for too long or is too strong, the three doshas can either become greater or smaller. The process of regulation is hindered, blocked or stimulated too much or too little.

According to the teachings of Ayurveda, the physical symptoms can emerge on six levels:

- Level 1:
  Because of negative inner (endogenous) and outer (exogenous) influences an energetic build-up of one or two doshas (accumulation) occurs.

- Level 2:
  The now existing unbalance of each of the doshas increases, as the influences that disturbed them do not disappear. Therefore the energetic power of one or of two doshas is increased (intensification).

- Level 3:
  The dosha-disorder, which up until now has been localised, begins to spread to other areas of the body. The

energetic power circulates and spreads (circulation).

- Level 4:
  The corresponding dosha fixes itself to a certain place in the body and the energetic power is deposited (localization).

- Level 5:
  In the areas of the body, in which the dosha has fixed itself, the first light symptoms of illness appear. In unfavourable circumstances these symptoms can lead to an acute outbreak of illness (manifestation).

- Level 6:
  If the self-healing powers cannot re-establish the balance, the acute health disorder can reach a chronic stage.

COMPLETE PRECAUTION AND CARE

In the complete teachings of Ayurveda the human being is considered as a whole, which means his consciousness, his body, his way of life and his environment. The two pillars of Ayurveda are health precautions and health care, as well as the strengthening of spiritual-intellectual and physical self-healing powers. According to this thousand year old Indian teaching each person can achieve lasting health through an individual, healthy way of life. Parts of this healthy way of life are the right diet, self-knowledge, an exten-

sion of consciousness and a respect for the laws of nature. If the inner balance is disturbed at all due to exogenous or endogenous influences then healing becomes the focal point instead of precaution and care. Because of its complete approach, Ayurveda is effective in healing chronic and psychosomatic illness, for which classical medicine from time to time does not offer a solution.

THE HEALTHY WAY

Learn through the Ayurvedic teaching how to recognize the nutritional and stress-related factors, which have led to an unbalance of your doshas. Counteract them and in the future, avoid them. Ayurveda will help you to change your life, so that you are considerably more content and balanced than before.

THE BASIS OF AYURVEDA: THE FIVE ELEMENTS AND THE THREE DOSHAS

Everything in the universe, human beings included, consists of energy (prahna). We are a bundle of energy waves, which are constantly changing. According to fundamental belief in Ayurveda we should live in such a way so that virtually all changes in energy have a positive effect on us, which means we must always support the balance of energy.

Happiness means that one does not suffer from a mental illness and possesses youth, strength, ability, knowledge and sense organs (eyes, nose, mouth, ears, skin) that function very well. When we have reached this state of happiness, all our efforts will be rewarded with success. One is able to plan one's life, as one would like it. Therefore the meaning of *happiness* differs in Ayurvedic teaching notably from that of our Western world. For us happiness does mean health, but it is also on a par with material values such as money, a house or a car.

THE MEANING OF LIFE

In Ayurveda life is defined as the unity of body, mind, soul and the sense organs. Only through this combination or this unity can life exist, according to Indian philosophy. According to Ayurvedic teachings, the meaning of life can be achieved through dahrma (virtue), artha (abundance), karma (joy) and moksa (relief). This can only be reached, however, when body and mind are healthy, which means that a balance exists between the three doshas.

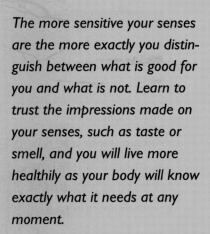

THE THEORY OF THE FIVE ELEMENTS

According to Ayurvedic philosophy, the universe consists of five eternal elements, namely:

- Space, ether
- Air
- Fire
- Water
- Earth

These five elements or also eternal elements are called mahabhutas in Ayurveda. They join themselves with the soul, in order to create life. These elements are contained in all things that live and do not live, as well as in our bodies. The composition of the five elements is defined by the individual and unmistakable character of each one. They determine the exceptional quality of the body, its weaknesses and strengths.

The following five qualities exist in the mahabhutas:

- Sapta (sound)
- Sparasa (touch)
- Hopa (sight)
- Java (taste)
- Ganha (smell)

Through our sense organs we are aware of these five qualities.

The five elements and the five qualities (i.e. senses) and sense organs are related to each other as follows:

- Space and sound
- Air and touch
- Fire and sight
- Water and taste
- Earth and smell

In human beings these five elements can be attributed to different areas of the body or functions. In this way, space corresponds to bodily cavities (mouth, nostrils, thorax, stomach, respiratory tract, cells). Air stands for muscle use, pulse, as well as the expansion and contraction of the lungs, and intestines. Even the movement of cells is associated with air. Fire controls the work of enzymes and drives the digestive system and metabolism. Water is found in blood, saliva, gastric juices, mucous membranes and in cell liquids. Earth embodies the solid structures of the body, such as bones, nails, teeth, muscles, cartilage, tendons, skin and hair.

THE THREE DOSHAS

Each person possesses a unique state of health, which is determined through the balance between the three energies of life, the three doshas. The Sanskrit names of the three doshas are Vata, Pitta and Kapha. According to Ayurvedic teaching they are the most important factors in the human organism and control our physic and our function. The three doshas are derived from the five elements, the mahabhutas.

The more sensitive your senses are the more exactly you distinguish between what is good for you and what is not. Learn to trust the impressions made on your senses, such as taste or smell, and you will live more healthily as your body will know exactly what it needs at any moment.

11

The three doshas are derived from the following combination of the five elements (mahabhutas).

🍃 Air and space result in Vata

🍃 Fire results in Pitta

🍃 Water and earth result in Kapha

HEALTH, BEHAVIOUR AND CHARACTER – THE THREE DOSHAS ARE RESPONSIBLE

For our health and our well-being it is important that your three doshas are in a state of balance. Only in this state of balance do they give us strength, good appearance, intact organs and also a long life. If the doshas lose their balance then an illness will develop.

The condition and behaviour of every person are determined by the three doshas, yet each of us can also be dominated by one or two doshas.

The doshas are not only responsible for our constitution and potentially occurring illnesses but also for our temperament, our hair colour, our stature and our diet. In this way the doshas influence all areas of our body and mind throughout our whole lives.

VATA, PITTA, KAPHA – THEY CONTROL FROM THE BEGINNING

Each dosha has its role within the organism. Vata embodies the driving force. It is linked with the nervous system and physical energy. Pitta symbolises fire. Therefore it is associated with metabolism, digestion, enzymes, acid and gallbladder. Kapha stands for water, which is found in mucous membrane, mucus, liquid, fat and in lymph vessels. Charaka, who is thought to be one of the first internists of Ayurvedic medicine and whose life is dated as being in the second century before Christ, wrote in his medical work: "Vata, Pitta and Kapha, in their balanced state, preserve the unity of the living human organism and blend in order to make the human being into a complete person, who can use his endriyas (sense organs) and is in possession of strength, good appearance and the certainty of a long life."

THE THREE DOSHAS DETERMINE CONSTITUTION

Already at the time of conception the three doshas of the parents determine the constitution of the growing human being. Each newly-born baby shows the status of prakruti. This means that the optimal balance of the three doshas for that particular person prevails at the time of birth. During the course of life this prakruti state changes into one of vikruti – the doshas lose their balance. Nutrition, environment, stress, traumas or injuries are responsible for this. If this unbalance is allowed to get out of control or lasts too long, illnesses can develop (see page 7). Ayurveda tries to bring back the individual prakuti state that was present at the time of birth.

Digestion is also controlled by the balance of the doshas. Therefore Pitta and Kapha aid digestion and Vata controls the movability of the intestines. As a result, a disturbance of balance between the doshas leads to stomach-bowel illnesses, such as constipation, diarrhoea, and flatulence or to a stomach ulcer. Other illnesses such as rheumatoid arthritis, arthrosis or asthma and bronchitis are also the result of a disturbance in the dosha balance.

The three energies, the three doshas, determine:

- Our outer physical phenotype
- The way our organs work
- The level of our intellectual abilities
- The individual make-up of our soul

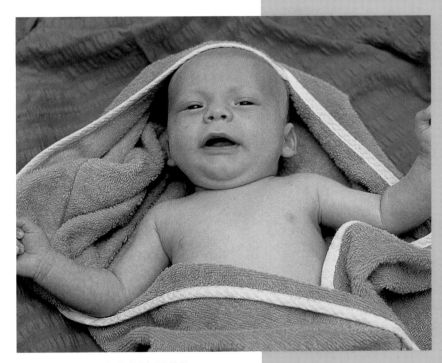

ONE DOSHA TYPE IS RARE

Each person can be categorised as being Vata, Pitta or Kapha, depending on his or her features. It is however seldom that a person is only of one type. In most people there are elements of two or even three doshas. Therefore there are not only three, but a total of seven different types of person:

- Vata-type
- Pitta-type
- Kapha-type
- Vata-Pitta-type
- Pitta-Kapha-type
- Vata-Kapha-type
- Vata-Pitta-Kapha-type

In Ayurveda there are no bad or good characteristics, they are judged as neutral. Each Ayurvedic type of constitution has strengths and weaknesses. When you know these strengths and weaknesses, you also know more about your vulnerability towards certain illnesses, the ideal diet, the most suitable climate as well as the best times of the year and the day. Therefore you learn more about how you should organise your way of life and how you relate to the environment.

Now we would like to describe the main types.

THE VATA-TYPE

The term Vata is also derived from the Sanskrit and means "to move oneself" or "to enthuse". In people of Vata-type both elements of space and air are domi-

nant. Vata is the strongest of the three doshas. It distributes itself through the

sense organs, the nervous system and body tissue. It is responsible for the transport of nutrition, for the removal of waste products from the body and for respiration.

People of the Vata-type mostly react extremely sensitively toward changes. They are very receptive to stimuli and are often over-wrought. They have a restless mind and have a bad memory. Their physical activity and their sensitiveness are reflected in their preference for sport and creative activities.

Sometimes Vata-people distinguish themselves by indulging in an excess of pleasures. That is why the most important requirement for the Vata-type is to find a regular rhythm in life and enough time for relaxation.

ILLNESSES THROUGH A DISTURBED VATA-DOSHA

80 different illnesses, according to Ayurvedic teaching, can be traced back to an unbalanced Vata. We will only mention the most important ones here. Because of his tendency to dryness, the Vata-type frequently has rough skin, brittle fingernails with grooves and a dry mouth. Rheuma-

The most important characteristics of the Vata-type at a glance

- *Low weight*
- *Small build*
- *Tendency to get dry skin*
- *Irregularly occurring feelings of hunger*
- *Irregular digestion*
- *Tendency to get constipation and flatulence*
- *Limited need for sleep*
- *Easily enthused*
- *Good short-term, bad long-term memory*
- *Often unsure and afraid*

14

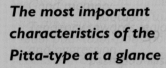

tism, aching joints, arthritis, constipation, heart disease, headaches, stomach problems and weight loss are typical signs of an unbalanced Vata-dosha. Likewise, tense muscles, heart complaints, feelings of dizziness and neuralgia can result.

Insomnia, anxiety, depression and agitation are some of the psychological problems of the Vata-type.

CAUSES OF AN UNBALANCED VATA-DOSHA

These Vata-unbalances are caused by certain types of behaviour. Firstly, there are over-activity and a lack of relaxation. But the Vata-dosha can also be brought out of balance by having too many emotional relationships without the adequate time to realise these feelings or to think about them, as well as a lack of emotional or familial support. Vata-unbalances are also triggered by cold, windy weather, by having too many leafy vegetables or other raw food and also by the absence of regularity and routine.

THE BALANCED VATA-DOSHA

A positive prevailing mood and balance are the marks of an undisturbed Vata-balance. Spontaneity and flexibility as well as a clear, alert mind point to a harmonious Vata-dosha.

THE PITTA-TYPE

Pitta is also a word from the Sanskrit and means "to heat up" or "to burn". Pitta controls all biochemical sequences in the body, including the production of heat. This dosha consists of the element of fire. The Pitta-dosha provides the body with colour, shine and warmth, as well as intellect, attentiveness and sight. Apart from that, it determines the feelings of hunger, thirst and taste.

People of the Pitta-type are intelligent and

precise, yet are often irritable. They easily sweat and therefore avoid high temperatures and sun.

ILLNESS THROUGH A DISTURBED PITTA-DOSHA

40 illnesses are caused by an unbalanced Pitta-dosha, for example fever or low

The most important characteristics of the Pitta-type at a glance

- Medium size and stature
- Normal, often freckled skin
- Blond, light brown or often reddish hair, which becomes prematurely grey
- Clear, but shrill speech
- Light but uninterrupted sleep
- High intelligence
- Good memory
- Tendency towards jealousy and aggression
- Large appetite
- Good digestion
- Prefers cold, sweet and sour and spicy foods

body temperature, deterioration of the skin in shine, colour and appearance, impaired sight, a burning sensation in the chest and in the whole body, sweating, hardening of the muscles, nettle rash, jaundice, mouth infections and conjunctiva infections. Insomnia, halitosis, bad digestion and skin disorders can also be blamed on an unbalanced Pitta.

Aggression, stubbornness and inconsiderateness are the signs of a Pitta unbalance on the soul-spirit level.

CAUSES OF AN UNBALANCED PITTA-DOSHA

The Pitta-dosha can become unbalanced due to the following ways of behaviour:

- Too warm or too many clothes on in high temperatures
- Too much heat
- Food too spicy
- Excess alcohol consumption
- Too little intake of liquid (water)
- Too little activity in the fresh air
- No steady, loving and secure relationship

THE UNBALANCED PITTA

Inner peace, satisfaction and balance are the characteristic signs of a stable Pitta-dosha. In this constellation the Pitta person reaches high energy levels, which boost his physical activity. Hot flushes or infections do not occur during this phase.

The functions of the Pitta are:

- *Sight*
- *Digestion*
- *Production of heat*
- *Pigmentation of the body*
- *Hunger, thirst, appetite*
- *Elasticity and suppleness of the body*
- *All intellectual skills*

THE KAPHA-TYPE

The Sanskrit word Kapha means "apathy" but also "to hug" or "to hold together". Kapha represents the source of strength and resistance. According to Ayurvedic teaching, Kapha is responsible for the build of the human body.

This dosha consists of the elements of water and earth. The combination of these elements also determines the distinctly more stable nature of Kapha, when com-

pared with the other two doshas.

Kapha gives a person strength, soft-heartedness and satisfaction. This dosha regulates the development of cells and function

of reproduction in the body. People who have a dominant Kapha possess a stable personality and distinguish themselves through having a lot of patience. Seldom

do they become angry. However, if they are angry, it is difficult to calm them down. Kapha people are honourable, stick to their word and do not lie. They talk slowly and can be lethargic and sometimes even lazy. They often have to be motivated by other people. Kapha generates determination, plumpness, enthusiasm, wisdom and ability.

THE UNBALANCED KAPHA-DOSHA

20 illnesses are caused by an unbalanced Kapha. Among them is, for example, anorexia, but also being overweight, excessive production of mucus, respiratory disorders such as colds, bronchitis or sinusitis, digestive disorders, arteriosclerosis, diabetes, goitre, obesity and nettle rash, as well as weakness, a tendency to become ill, impotence and sterility. Insomnia, an excessive need for sleep as well as laziness and a lack of energy indicate that the Kapha-dosha is unbalanced. On the soul-spirit level, an unbalanced Kaphadosha often leads to a lack of energy and to depression.

CAUSES OF AN UNBALANCED KAPHA-DOSHA

An unbalanced Kapha-dosha is caused by:

- Too little physical activity
- A lethargic way of life
- Excessive intake of sweet foods or drinks
- Too much sleep
- Too many and too heavy meals
- Cold food and drink
- Wet weather
- damp clothing
- too much dependency on partner

THE BALANCED KAPHA-DOSHA

If a balance exists between the water and the earth element the Kapha-type will show physical strength. He has powerful limbs and has a well-proportioned body. Sympathy, leniency, courage, vitality and psychological stability are characteristic of him.

The most important characteristics of the Kapha-type at a glance

- *Strong build*
- *Often overweight*
- *Pale, patchy, greasy skin*
- *Thick, wavy, very dark or very light hair*
- *Great need for sleep*
- *Slow intelligence*
- *Good memory*
- *Constant appetite*
- *Quiet and secure*
- *Seldom irritable*
- *Potentially greedy and possessive*

The most important functions of Kapha

- *Maintenance of suppleness in the body and of the organs*
- *Preservation of physical stability*
- *Creation of energy, patience and strength*
- *Ensuring elasticity of limbs*
- *Leniency, courage, generosity*

17

THE CLASSIFICATION OF THE THREE DOSHAS – SELF-ANALYSIS

As Ayurveda divides people into seven different types of constitution, it details their changeable needs and adapts itself perfectly to their varying requirements.

Each person is, of course, unique. Because of this uniqueness it seems almost impossible to put people into certain categories. Therefore Ayurvedic medicine relies on classification according to physical build or behaviour patterns, for example, in order to obtain information about possible disorders in the dosha balance. For this reason a test has been developed, a type of questionnaire, which will help you to recognise yourself and to get to know your personal strengths and weaknesses.

Take your time to fill in this questionnaire, yet give your answers spontaneously. Through this test you will find out which pure or mixed dosha-type you are.

This knowledge will help you to understand better your actions and reactions in certain situations, to take specific action against certain illnesses and to take special measures towards health provision.

The following three questionnaires are designed for each type of dosha and consist of about 60 statements, which you can judge according to three different categories: does not apply, sometimes applies, and applies most.

The points scale ranges from 0 to 6. The stronger a statement applies to you, the higher the mark that you should give it. Should you have problems answering a question, focus your points on how you have felt in the last few years. Do not forget that you can also possess the characteristics of more than one dosha.

When you have answered all the questions, add the points together from each questionnaire. Then compare the numbers of points with each other. In this way you can recognise, whether one dosha or two doshas predominate in you, or whether all three doshas are as strongly characterised as each other. The dosha, which has the highest number of points, is the dominant one for you.

THE VATA-TEST

	Does not apply		Sometimes applies			Applies most	
	0	1	2	3	4	5	6
Quick, light walk			✓				
Lack of decision			✓				
Tendency to get flatulence and constipation			✓				
Quickly gets cold hands and feet	✓						
Anxious and afraid		✓					
Aversion to cold weather		✓					
Fast speech, very chatty				✓			
Tendency to mood swings, emotional reactions			✓	✓			
Difficulty falling asleep and sleeping			✓		✓		
Tendency to get dry skin, especially in winter			✓				
Active mind, imaginative, restless					✓		
Performs activities quickly						✓	
Bad long-term memory, not good at memorizing	✓		✓				
Lively and enthusiastic					✓		
Slim physique, no tendency to put on weight			✓				
Learns things easily				✓			
Quick movements, lots of activity, sudden energy bursts			✓		✓		
Easily excitable				✓			
Irregular sleeping and eating habits				✓			
Aversion to draughts					✓		

2   16   15   20   5

22

(64)

THE PITTA-TEST

	Does not apply		Sometimes applies			Applies most	
	0	1	2	3	4	5	6
...h, silky, thin, red or red-... ...air, which quickly goes grey	✓						
...d appetite						✓	
...dency to be stubborn				✓			
...gular digestion and tendency ...o get diarrhoea		✓					
Not very patient		✓		✓			
Tendency to perfectionism		✓					
Easily angered, but not unforgiving			✓ ✓				
Preference for cold foods and drinks				✓		✓	
Very direct and extrovert manner				✓			
Intolerance of spicy and hot foods		✓ ✓					
Works efficiently					✓		
Accurate and focussed behaviour		✓ ✓					
Strong will and good ability to assert oneself		✓		✓		✓	
Aversion to damp, warm weather	✓						
Sweats easily	✓						
Quick to become irritable and angry, but not visibly			✓ ✓				
Missing meals leads to unbalance		✓ ✓					
Tolerance is not very great				✓			
Seeks a challenge, very determined				✓ ✓			
Tendency to self-criticism and criticism				✓ ✓			

8   10   18   4   18

(55)

THE KAPHA-TEST

	Does not apply		Sometimes applies			Applies most	
	0	1	2	3	4	5	6
Slow and deliberate behaviour		✓		✓			
Seldom loses self-control					✓		
Good long-term memory, however learning difficult			✓	✓			
No financial problems		✓					
Aversion to cold, damp weather		✓					
Wavy, dark and thick hair		✓		✓			
Pale, smooth and soft skin		✓					
Large, solid body build						✓	
Cheerful, loving and tender nature, not unforgiving			✓		✓		
Easily gains weight, difficult to lose weight			✓			✓	
Placid and calm disposition				✓		✓	
No discomfort at skipping meals		✓					
Tendency to get asthma, chronic constipation, mucous congestion or lethargy	✓					✓	
Great need for sleep				✓			
Deep sleep				✓			
Regular digestion		✓					
Good stamina, physical endurance and a steady level of energy				✓	✓		
Slow and measured walk			✓				
Oversleeps, slow to wake up			✓			✓	
Slow and methodical action, also when eating			✓				

34

12 12 15 30 10
6 (69,8) 4 20

THE THREE GUNAS

...e three gunas –
...e and unbalance

...nparison to the three
...hich can all slip out of
...ce, this is only possible
...wo gunas, namely rajas
...mas. On the other hand
...purpose of the third guna,
...tva, is to maintain balance
and consistency.

As the three doshas represent the foundation of our physical condition, so do the three gunas, sattva, rajas and tamas, form similarly the functional qualities of our mind. According to Ayurvedic teaching, our characteristics are determined genetically. They are determined by the dominance of one of the three gunas. In every person there is a certain mixture of these three characteristics but the dominant guna defines the psychological constitution as a sattva, rajas or tamas constitution.

As with the three doshas, the three gunas also ensure a balanced equilibrium for a healthy mind. If the gunas come out of balance it can lead to different mental problems. It is interesting that only two of the gunas, rajas and tamas can lose their balance, for example through stress or negative characteristics such as yearning (kama), malice (irsya), delusion and hallucination (moha), greed (lobha), anxiety (sinta), fear (bhaya) and rage (karodha). In comparison the guna, sattva, is pure and cannot become unbalanced.

SATTVA

Sattva can be described as light, awareness, joy and clarity. It is free of illness. The presence of sattva is necessary for the functioning of our senses. Apart from that, sattva is responsible for the acquisition of knowledge. Among the characteristic features of the sattva person is the inability to lie. People of the sattva type are always honest. Selflessness and sympathy come first. Their weaknesses are pride and a lack of humility. Sattva people work hard and selflessly in order to help others. They show noble and spiritual characteristics. In the physical constitution of a sattva person one often finds a mostly Kapha element either as the dominant dosha or in combination with other doshas: Kapha-Pitta, Pitta-Kapha, Kapha-Vata, Vata-Kapha.

Sattva people can be divided into seven sub-types:

Brahma
This type lacks weaknesses such as passion, rage, greed, ignorance or jealousy. He is characterised by knowledge and a distinct power of discernment.

Arva
One searches in vain here too for weaknesses such as pride, egoism, ignorance, greed and rage. Instead one finds understanding, reserve, refinement, love and self-control, as well as an excellent memory.

Ayindra
Spiritual knowledge and interests come first with this person. Virtue, courage and foresight belong to his characteristic features.

Yamya
Emotional ties, hate, envy and ignorance are unknown to these people. They have an excellent memory, are energetic and have leadership qualities.

Varuna
Sattva people of this type express their feelings at the appropriate time. Religious rites are important to them.

Kabera
Courage, patience, virtue and purity are characteristic for sattva people of this type. They love rest and relaxation. They hate impure thoughts.

Gandarva
This type is considerably different from the other six sub-categories. These people are often rich and love luxury. They know a lot about poetry, prose and literature. People of this type are full of passion; they love dance, song and music as well as good perfume and flowers.

RAJAS

Rajas is the most active of the three gunas. Desire, wishes, ambition and inconstancy can be related to rajas. Rajas people have an angrier manner. They work very hard but otherwise do not look on the bright side of life. In fact they are not insincere and do not hurt others knowingly, but in order to save their own skin, they resort to white lies. Rajas people have a talent for business. They can evaluate very well the strengths and weaknesses of their partner or business partner. Therefore one finds in this group many successful business people. Rajas people have

a high intellect, are however an easy target for the temptations in life.

They are dominated either by Pitta or have an element of Pitta in their personality: Pitta-Kapha, Kapha-Pitta, Pitta-Vata, Vata-Pitta.

There are six different rajas sub-categories:

Assora
High-handedness, cruelty, envy and also inconsiderateness characterise this sub-type of person, who often puts on an act. Courage is one of his strengths.

An Ayurvedic doctor can find out nearly everything about a patient's state of health through the ten-part examination.

AYURVEDIC MEDICATION

In Ayurvedic medicine the medications are divided into three groups: products of vegetable, animal and mineral origin.

The animal products are honey, wax and fat. Gold, silver, copper, precious stones, iron and chalk belong to the mineral medications.

The Ayurvedic medications are nearly always used in a combination. They are available as ointments, powder, juice, liquid, tablets and oils.

As in western medicine, the Ayurvedic medications have to be taken at certain times of the day. In Ayurvedic medicine the so-called ten-rule shows when medications have to be taken, in order for them give their strongest effect.

The following dosage times and dosage variations are given in the ten-rule:

- On an empty stomach
- Before meals
- After meals
- Between meals
- During a meal
- Mixing a medication into food
- At the beginning and at the end of a meal
- Several times daily
- With every mouthful of a meal
- With every second mouthful of a meal

PURIFYING HEALING METHODS

In Ayurveda complete health means a balance between the energies of life Vata, Pitta and Kapha (see page 11ff.). Therefore, to establish a harmony between these three doshas is of principle importance in all health and healing methods in Ayurveda. To balance the three doshas, Ayurveda allows for three courses of action, which are, however, not intended to be used on their own, but which can only lead to the desired success through their combination and working together. It is about:

- Detoxification or purification
- Regeneration
- Nutrition

DETOXIFICATION WITH PANCHAKARMA

Panchakarma is a word from the Indian scholar language, Sanskrit. Translated into English it means the "five actions". The term summarises the five main groups of physical therapeutic procedure in Ayurveda. The healing powers, from which they arise, follow a logical order and compliment one another.

Above all the following complaints respond well to Ayurvedic treatments:

- *Allergies*
- *Anxiety*
- *Eye disorders*
- *Bronchitis*
- *Eczema, skin problems*
- *Colds*
- *High blood pressure*
- *Sinusitis*
- *Irritability*
- *Rheumatoid arthritis*
- *Back problems*
- *Insomnia*
- *Stress*
- *Digestion problems*

35

Important!

Each detoxification should only be carried out by a trained Ayurvedic therapist. On no account should you try to use panchakarma at home. Above all, particular caution is needed with children and pregnant women. Also with some existing illnesses not all the steps of panchakarma can be carried out. In this case you should consult your Ayurvedic doctor.

In this way a lasting and intensive thorough purification is achieved. Introduced below are the three steps in treatment, which make it possible for us through panchakarma to systematically remove harmful substances and bodily poisons, which easily accumulate in the body through having the wrong train of thought, environmental pollution or an unsuitable way of life.

With the help of these three steps the state of health can improve. Those who are chronically ill can often relieve their disorders in this way; fully healthy people gain additional joie de vivre and contentment through a treatment.

- First step

    At the beginning of the treatment the organism is given either externally or internally easily digested healing oils. In this way, metabolism is stimulated and the effectiveness of digestion is aided. The internal oil treatment can be carried out through taking pure butterfat, for example ghee or other substances.

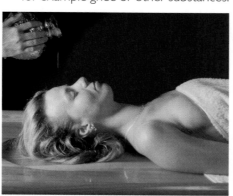

These go via the intestine directly into the body cells. Externally, this treatment is done through pouring oil over the whole body.

In this way, environmental poisons and fat-soluble metabolic waste can be removed in an effective and uncomplicated way.

- Second step

    The next step in treatment includes a pleasant use of heat such as an herbal steam bath, hot compresses or a rubdown. Warmth widens blood and lymph vessels and again, increases metabolic activity.

    This application ensures that the previously dissolved bodily poisons and environmental toxins are washed out of the vessels and therefore take their natural route into the intestine.

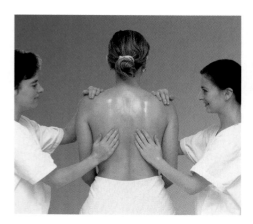

- Third step

    This phase of treatment ensures that the previously dissolved toxins irrevocably leave the body. The intestine is pleasantly purified through a careful laxative effect and soft enemas – the waste products therefore finally leave the body.

EXTERNAL PURIFICATION WITH MASSAGES

Panchakarma does for the external purification what it does for internal detoxification, but through regular massages. The massages can be carried out at home in the form of self-massage as part of your morning toilet.

OIL MASSAGE

Not only does the body (nerves, muscles, digestion) profit from oil massage, but also mind and soul.

Sesame seed oil for massage

In Ayurveda, a quality high-grade, virgin sesame seed oil is prescribed. Only people of the Pitta type or with skin disorders may switch to olive or coconut oil. Sesame seed oil for the massage must be prepared beforehand. Heat it in a saucepan to about 110°C, not higher. The oil becomes thinner and runnier and is absorbed better into the skin. Apart from that, it can also be kept for longer after cooling down. One can keep the "ripe" sesame seed oil in a dark, glass bottle. Before using the oil for a massage, you should gently heat the required amount of oil in a water bath.

How often to massage?

People of the Vata type should massage themselves daily. On the other hand, with Kapha and Pitta people it is sufficient when a massage is part of the routine two or three times a week.

The ideal time for an oil massage is in the morning, after a shower. It is best to sit on a chair or on a warm floor and put a towel under yourself. Cover your whole body in oil, but only as much as you need to be able to massage the skin well. Massage using stroking and circling movements. Stroking movements are used for the upper and lower arms as well as for thighs, calves and back. With circling movements you should massage the joints as well as the chest and stomach.

If you do not have time in the morning for a whole body massage, you could also do one in the evening. However, you should remember then to massage yourself before eating. Alternatively, you can carry out partial massages, for example on the face, ears, hands and feet. It will take less time but will have the same beneficial effect. It is important that you are loose and relaxed for all oil massages.

- **Head**
  Slowly massage the scalp with your fingertips in circling movements. Start with the hairline at the front and then go to the sides and to the nape of the neck.

- **Ears**
  Massage both ears at the same time with gentle movements forwards and backwards.
- **Forehead**
  Massage the forehead with fingertips. Do stroking movements from the middle of the forehead to the outer part. Finish the forehead massage by

doing circling movements on the temples.

- **Nape of the neck and neck**
  Rub up and down in the direction of the hairline with both hands left and right of the shoulders. Just stroke the front of the neck gently from top to bottom.

🍂 Chin

Massage from the cheeks to the chin with fingertips in circling movements. Then massage there exactly as for the forehead. Finally, stroke gently left and right along the nose with both index fingers.

🍂 Arms

Using strong pressure, rub the upper and lower arms with up and down movements, first the right and then the left arm. Massage the joints with a circling movement. Begin at the shoulder

and finish by holding the fingers one at a time and gently massaging them in the direction of the fingernails.

🍂 Chest

Massage the chest gently with circling movements. Women should massage around the breast. Carefully massage the breastbone with up and down movements.

🍂 Stomach

Stroke the stomach with the right palm in a clockwise circle.

🍂 Legs

Treat the legs the same as the arms. Massage the right and then the left leg. Carry out circling movements on the joints.

🍂 Back and bottom

Stand up straight and massage the lower part of the back with the palms in strong upward and downward movements. This also applies to the bottom.

🍂 Feet

The body massage finishes with a foot massage.

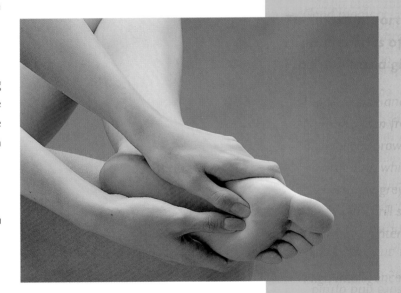

39

Massage the toes one by one. Massaging the back and the sole of the foot finishes the foot massage.

After the massage you should allow 10 to 15 minutes, as it does not take long for the oil to be absorbed fully into the skin. You can wash off the oil with a mild soap in a warm bath or warm shower.

DRY MASSAGE

The dry massage is carried out using special gloves made out of rough or burette silk. You can obtain these gloves from an Ayurvedic retail outlet.
As the dry massage strongly stimulates the circulation, metabolism and connective tissue it is most suitable for people with greasy skin, metabolism problems or who are overweight. A dry massage is also good for joint complaints, such as chronic arthritis, and for cellulite. Unlike the oil massage, people of the Kapha type can

The dry massage can be carried out daily by Kapha people.

have a dry massage daily. A final hot bath stimulates the purifying effect of the dry massage.

MASSAGE BY A THERAPIST

If you would like to treat yourself once in a while, spoil yourself with one of the three basic types of Ayurvedic massage. These massages are offered in Ayurvedic centres and also by Ayurvedic therapists.

- Abhyanga
  For this whole body massage the masseur uses different types of oil that suit your type of constitution – Vata, Pitta or Kapha. The masseur employs a combination of different hand movements, for example, pressing, kneading, rubbing or tapping. The abhyanga is always followed by an herbal sauna. The massage lasts between 30 and 60 minutes. It has a relaxing and calming effect.

- Pizzichil
  During this very special form of massage the masseurs work with gentle stroking movements. During this, warm oil is constantly dripped onto the body. This type of massage is normally carried out by at least four people. Two drip oil onto the body, while two massage at the same time. This massage stimulates the metabolism through the skin and organs. It is important that a doctor is always present for this massage.

MOUTHWASH (GANDHUSA)

🐾 Chawuzetti pizzichil
This type of Ayurvedic massage might seem very exotic to us. Here the masseur not only uses his hands as tools but also the soles of his feet. For this he hangs from a hook on the ceiling. One needs one or more masseurs and two or more assistants for this massage. The assistants pour oil onto the patient at certain intervals.

The same sesame seed oil, which is used for the whole body massage (see page 37), can be used for the mouthwash.

🐾 Rinse the oral cavity, throat and particularly the gums with a teaspoon of sesame seed oil for two to three minutes. Suck the oil through the teeth. Spit out the oil afterwards. The gums are strengthened through this mouthwash, and the resistance to disease-causing agents is improved.

REGENERATION THROUGH THE THREE-DOSHA-EXERCISES AND YOGA

According to Ayurvedic teachings, regeneration means re-establishing and strengthening the balance of the doshas. This can be achieved with the help of relaxing, meditative exercises. If you carry out the exercises consistently and regularly, balance and contentment will become apparent. It is easier to overcome daily stress situations.

Healthy movement, for example walks in the fresh air or special physical activities are very important in Ayurveda. The purpose of this movement is to bring mind and body into line with each other. Of

For the Kapha type, fencing, dancing, running, football, tennis, rowing and weight training are recommended.

course, one can do many types of sport, whereby you should be aware that not every sport is equally suitable for every type of constitution.

People of the Vata type should add yoga, aerobics, walking, short rambles and cycling to their list of preferred sports.

For the Pitta type, swimming, rambling, riding, sailing and also skiing and rock-climbing are suitable.

THE THREE-DOSHA-EXERCISES

The so-called three-dosha exercises play an important role in Ayurvedic teachings. One understands by them the fundamental movements, which support the balance of Vata, Pitta and Kapha and which consist of the "Sun Salute", light yoga and simple breathing exercises.

THE SUN SALUTE

The Sun Salute (Surya Namaskara) consists of twelve positions, which should be done one after the other without interruption.

In total this exercise lasts about one to two minutes, in the beginning a bit longer. You will soon notice that when you complete the Sun Salute consistently every day, the muscles relax and the joints become more moveable. Furthermore, the Sun Salute acts as a massage for the internal organs and stimulates circulation and flow of blood.

In the course of time, you will notice how body and mind are melting into one unit.

First position:
The Salutation position

Stand up straight, do not stretch out legs completely, have feet parallel to each other; fold your hands in front of your chest, arms bent.

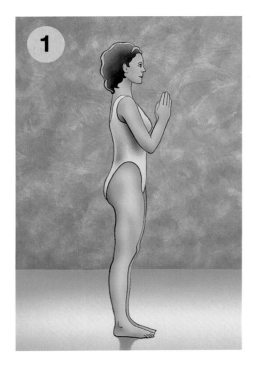

Second position:
Lifting arms

Breath in through the nose, slowly raise arms over the head, stretch the upper body, whereby the spine bends back-

Morning is the best time

For any movement training an hour after the morning shower is the most appropriate. Complete the exercises before breakfast. Allow enough time for each cycle. Only increase the speed of the exercises gradually, above all, if you have hardy done any sporting activity up until now. Only then are you able to prevent pulled or stretched muscles.

43

During each position you should breathe in and out calmly and steadily.

wards, and look upwards, continuing to breath steadily and stay in this position for a few seconds.

Third position: Hand to foot

Breathe out through the mouth and, at the same time, bend the upper body forwards with a straight spine as far as possible, stretch legs and touch the floor with hands; bend knees slightly. This exercise is usually quite hard at the beginning. However, you will notice that joints are becoming more flexible as time goes on.

serves as a support, whereby your foot stays firmly on the floor. The spine is straight, let your arms hang and look up to the ceiling.

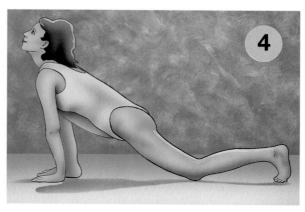

Fifth position: The mountain position

With the next exhalation put your palms on the floor, stretch your right leg behind as well, and put next to the left leg. Raise your bottom and hips, the heels press firmly on the floor, stretch the back of the legs.

Fourth position: The equestrian position

During the next inhalation, slowly go into a squat, stretching the left leg straight out behind you, until the knee touches the floor. Do not stretch your right leg; it

Sixth position The eight limbs position

As you are exhaling, the knees gradually touch the floor, the body sinks into a

stretched position until the chest and chin also go onto the floor. In this position all eight points of the body, namely the chin, chest, hands, knees and toes are in contact with the floor.

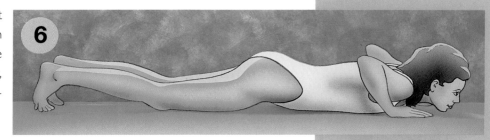

Seventh position:
The cobra position

When inhaling, stretch the thorax and with hands pressing on the floor, push head and body upwards, leaving the pelvis on the floor. While pushing the upper body upwards, slowly bend your head behind the nape of the neck.

Eighth position:
The mountain position

When exhaling, push the bottom upwards, keeping feet firmly on the floor (see position 5).

Ninth position:
The equestrian position

With the next inhalation, pull the left leg forward and bend, stretch the right leg behind you, the knee touching the floor (see position 4).

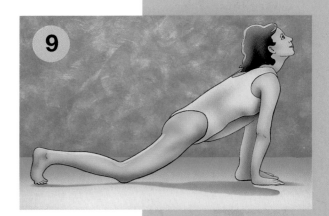

Tenth position: Hand to foot

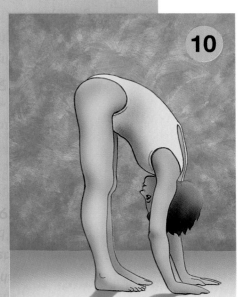

On exhaling put the right leg forward and move the bottom slowly upwards until the legs and spine are stretched. The spine, head and arms form a line (see position 3).

Eleventh position: Raised arms

When inhaling stretch both arms upwards at the same time. Make sure that the straightening up is initiated not from the head or the neck but from the upper back and the pelvis. Stretch the thorax, look upwards, breathe calmly and steadily (see position 2).

Twelfth position The rest position

Breathe out, let the arms drop, fold the hands in front of the chest, place both feet hip-width apart and stand up straight. As the thorax rises and sinks look forward. This exercise finishes the cycle of the Sun Salute. Before you start the cycle again you

should stand still for a few moments.

YOGA

Yoga is about science as well as about practical application. The principal goal of asana ("taking a comfortable position") and pranayama (respiratory control) is total health. Apart from that, it is seen as aiding inner strength in order to counteract daily stress in a peaceful and calm way.

Rishis and Maharishis, important holy and wise men, were the founders and developers of yoga in India thousands of years ago. Great importance is attached to yoga in Ayurveda. The word yoga was derived from the Sanskrit root "yuga", which means "to congregate" or "to unite". According to Ayurvedic teachings a person reaches a state of peace through yoga exercises, as does his inner balance. Yoga belongs to the basis of Ayurveda.

CLASSICAL EXERCISES

In Ayurveda Yoga is used in a therapeutic way as well as for staying healthy. We would like to introduce you here to five important positions, which are called asana. Please do not forget to avoid overtaxing your body with these exercises. Do the exercises slowly. Seek advice about them or instruction in the exercises from an experienced Ayurvedic therapist.

- The locust pose
  Sit cross-legged on the floor with your hands resting on your knees and the palms of your hands facing upwards. Breathe calmly and slowly.

- The head to knee pose
  From the sitting position, stretch out your legs and bend the right leg. Put the sole of your right foot against the inner thigh of the stretched leg. Now stretch the arms upwards, while

breathing in, and bend the body over the stretched-out leg when breathing out, until your forehead touches your knee. If you find this difficult, you could bend the stretched-out knee a little. Try to keep your back straight. After a few breaths come out of the pose and carry it out on the other side.

THE AYURVEDIC DIET

As with all rules in Ayurveda, the Ayurvedic recommendations do not apply to everyone equally. What might agree well with one person could mean the exact opposite for others. It can also be the case with two people of the same type of constitution that the same foods do not agree equally with them. The reason for this lies in the different division of the three doshas. Talk about your diet with an experienced Ayurvedic doctor. When you add new foods to your diet, you should start by eating them in small quantities.

According to Ayurvedic teachings – and not just them – the right diet is the keystone for general health. Food also plays a big role in the western world, yet seldom do we really take the time to eat in a peaceful and relaxed atmosphere. Things usually look quite different: a quick snack on the side, a quick cup of coffee while working and a brief visit to the snack bar at midday to eat a hotdog or a hamburger standing up. Then, because of a guilty conscience as it were, we try to balance out the resulting deficit of vital nutrients, caused by our unhealthy and hectic style of diet, with vitamin and mineral tablets. The Ayurvedic teachings show us how easy it is to eat healthily and sensibly, without having to subject ourselves to a strict diet.

THE TASTE DECIDES

Food, in Ayurveda, depends on a very simple principle – our subjective taste –, which is contrary to our western culture, which divides food into fat, carbohydrates, protein, minerals, trace elements and vitamins. According to Ayurvedic teachings, the body knows what is good for it. Just as the organism regulates temperature, metabolism blood pressure, hormones and the

nervous system, it is in a position to indicate its needs to us.

Every one of us knows how it feels when the body is longing for a certain type of food. For example, you want something sour when you have eaten a lot of sweet things. After an evening of indulging in too much alcohol the body indicates through thirst that it would like to wash out toxins and needs water to do this.

INCLUDE
THE SENSES

In Ayurveda each food represents a treat for the senses. Calorie counts and nutritional tables do not play anywhere near the role that they do for us. The Ayurvedic diet focuses on our five senses, mainly on taste. Expressed differently: we can neither see nor taste fat, vitamins, minerals, trace elements, protein and carbohydrates. We do not notice them. If you bite into an apple, for example, which is classified in our western dietetics as being very healthy, you only eat it for its typical aroma and taste. We can say whether or not we like the taste of the apple.

And if we are honest: we do not actually plan our meals according to the latest scientific knowledge; rather we plan according to our preferences and dislikes.

This is exactly the starting point taken in Ayurveda. We should listen to our bodies and savour food with all our senses. However, a change in eating habits is necessary in order to stick to the diet rules in Ayurveda that relate to the different types of constitution. Of course, you cannot simply give up immediately the eating habits that you have had for a long time, be it the midday hotdog at the snack stand on the corner or the two cups of coffee in the morning. Try to do things slowly. Be patient. Gradually reduce the amounts of food that are unsuitable, according to Ayurveda. For example, reduce your coffee intake from two to one cup. Dilute this one cup with a lot of milk and water, and soon you will notice that you can do without coffee altogether. You should act similarly with regard to the consumption of meat. Although a vegetarian diet is recommended in Ayurveda, all types of meat are recognised and one knows which are suitable for each type of constitution. Try to restrict slowly your intake of meat. Instead of beef, pork or veal, eat poultry or fish more often.

Dieticians have now realised that starvation diets or yo-yo dieting are not healthy and are not appropriate for lasting weight loss. Instead of fasting for days on end, you should use one day in the week for purification by taking in liquids only, for example warm water, soups or teas.

THE AYURVEDIC DIET RULES

- Take your time to eat. Concentrate on each meal. Do not talk too much while eating.

- Take your meals in a relaxed atmosphere.

- Avoid eating quickly or while standing.

- Make your meals look appetising as all five senses savour the food.

- You should stick to a certain rhythm regarding the times of meals. Always try to take your meals at the same time, if possible.

- Not only your appetite but also your hunger decides whether or not you should eat something. Only when you really feel hungry, and the last meal was between three and six hours ago, should you eat something.

- Take your main meal at midday.

- In the evening you should only eat light foods. As food is not digested well during the night and puts a strain on circulation, you should not eat anything before going to bed.

- It is best to drink hot water with meals. Juice and herbal tea are also allowed. On the other hand, you should not drink milk with meals; only drink it on its own.

- Make sure that the food is warm. This facilitates digestion. Cold foods and drinks impair the agni.

- Abstain altogether from alcohol, coffee, carbonated drinks and chocolate.

- As sour dairy products, raw fruit and vegetables and animal protein are hard to digest, you should eliminate such foods from your evening meals.

- Eat oily foods, which means adding butter or ghee (see page 56) to your meals. This aids digestion and improves the appearance.

- Make sure that you only eat foods that really go together. Avoid the following combinations: honey – hot water, milk – fish, milk – garlic.

- Only eat until your stomach is a third full, therefore a third food, a third liquid. The last third is air.

- After eating, rest for a few moments before you start work again.

- When possible, eat your meals fresh. Avoid re-heated food.

THE SIX FLAVOURS (RASAS)

Give preference to foods from your local area. Eat these when they are available at the market.

Trust the needs of your body. Your appetite for certain dishes reflects the needs of your body.

Taste plays a central role in the Ayurvedic style of eating. There six different flavours know in Ayurveda, namely sweet, salty, sour, spicy, bitter and astringent. Ideally each meal should contain all six flavours, therefore all six rasas. This combination has a positive effect on the balance of the three doshas: Vata, Pitta and Kapha.

SWEET

We spontaneously associate the sweet taste with sugar. Yet fruit or cereals can also taste sweet. Sweet foods stimulate the pancreas. In Ayurveda the sweet foods include: different types of cereal, for example, barley, oats, rye, wheat; fruit (bananas, pears, figs, oranges, grapes etc); different types of vegetable, for example peas, cucumbers, cabbage, lentils, onions; sweet dairy products; castor-, olive-, sesame seed and sunflower oil; nuts such as hazel nuts, peanuts, coconut and walnuts; butter, ghee; potatoes, rice; meat; honey and sugar.

Ghee

Ghee is a type of clarified butter, which is easily digestible. In Ayurvedic cuisine ghee is used for steaming and baking, but also for improving foods. You can buy ghee in Ayurvedic retail outlets.

Please remember that this is simply about recommendations and guidance. You can obtain detailed information from an Ayurveda centre and from experienced Ayurveda doctors. A special dietary plan will be worked out for you there.

THE VATA-TYPE

The dominant element of the Vata-type is air with the characteristics of lightness, coldness, dryness, rawness, clarity and rapidity. These characteristics are balanced out through heavy, oily and warm foods. Therefore, soups and vegetable stews, for example, dampen this dosha, as well as fresh bread, pasta, rice or warm milk. On the other hand, the Vata-dosha is stimulated through cold meals like salad or drinks and raw vegetables. As a Vata-type, give preference to foods that taste salty, sour and sweet. As a Vata-type, you

should also make sure you have regular meals and take them in a relaxed atmosphere.

Suitable foods for Vata-types are:
Eggs: boiled eggs or scrambled egg
Meat: poultry, fish
Vegetables: cucumber, green beans, garlic, carrots, okra, beetroot, asparagus, sweet potatoes, white radish, onions (but not raw). The following are also suitable in moderate amounts: peas, potatoes, celery, spinach, tomatoes and courgettes. Cook vegetables and add some ghee to them.
Grains: basmati rice, wheat
Pulses: Chickpeas, mung beans, red lentils
Herbs and spices: aniseed, basil, estragon, fennel, fresh coriander, ginger, cardamom, cumin, caraway seeds, bay leaves, marjoram, mace, cloves, oregano, sage, black pepper, mustard, liquorice, thyme, juniper, cinnamon

Dairy products: above all butter, cream cheese, ghee, yoghurt, milk, cream

Nuts, seeds: all nuts and types of seed are suitable.

Fruit: pineapple, apricots, avocados, bananas, berries, fresh figs, grapefruit, honeydew melons, mangos, nectarines, papayas, peaches, plums, oranges, grapes, lemons. Fruit should be sweet and ripe.

Oils: all salad or cooking oils are suitable.

Sweeteners: maple syrup, honey, sugar cane products

The following are not suitable for the Vata type:

Meat: beef and pork

Vegetables: aubergines, cauliflower, broccoli, peppers, mushrooms, Brussels sprouts, red cabbage, bean sprouts, white cabbage. Avoid raw vegetables and salad.

Grains: buckwheat, barley, oats (uncooked), millet, maize, rye

Pulses: all except those mentioned above

Fruit: pears, pomegranates, cranberries, dried fruit, unripe bananas

Sweeteners: honey and white sugar in large amounts

THE PITTA-TYPE

The Pitta-type is defined through the elements of fire and water, whose qualities are lightness, heat, oiliness, spiciness, liquid and sourness. Pitta people very much like eating. They prefer sweet, bitter and astringent dishes. They have a nearly unquenchable thirst, especially in the summer. The Pitta-dosha can be dampened through cold, rich food and drinks. As a Pitta type, you should avoid salt; strong, spicy meals and oil, especially during the summer months. Eat a lot of salad. Make sure that you take your meals regularly.

The following foods are suitable for Pitta-types:

Eggs: egg white

Meat: pheasant, poultry, rabbit and game

Vegetables: cucumber, green beans, green leaf vegetables, green salad, chicory, potatoes, okra, peppers, mushrooms, Brussels sprouts, red cabbage, asparagus, bean sprouts, celery, white cabbage, courgettes

Grains: barley, oats, white rice (basmati rice), wheat

Pulses: fresh peas, green beans, chickpeas, mung beans, soya products (tofu)

Herbs, spices: only in small amounts: dill, fennel, turmeric (curcuma), fresh coriander, ginger, cardamom, mint, saffron, black pepper, cinnamon

Dairy products: butter (unsalted), ice cream, ghee, cottage cheese, milk

Nuts, seeds: coconut, pumpkin seeds, sunflower seeds

Fruit: apples, pineapples, avocados, pears, figs, coconuts, mangos, melons, oranges, plums, raisins, grapes, prunes. Fruit should be sweet and ripe.

Oils, fats: coconut, olive, soya, sunflower oil, ghee

Sweeteners: all sweeteners, with the exception of honey and molasses

The following foods are not suitable for Pitta-types:

Eggs: egg yolk

Meat: beef and pork, seafood

Vegetables: aubergines, carrots, radishes, beetroot, spicy peppers, spinach, tomatoes

Grains: brown rice, buckwheat, millet, maize, rye

Spices: aniseed, cayenne pepper, chilli, vinegar, ketchup, garlic, caraway seeds, cloves, pepper, salt, mustard grains, onions

Pulses: lentils, red lentils

Diary products: all sour dairy products

Nuts, seeds: cashew nuts, sesame seeds

Fruit: all sour fruit

Sweeteners: honey and molasses

THE KAPHA-TYPE

The elements of Kapha are water and earth. Therefore, its qualities are heaviness, coldness, oiliness, slowness, sliminess, thickness, softness, static and sweetness. Kapha people usually possess a healthy appetite. They prefer bitter and spicy tastes. The Kapha-dosha is strengthened through cold, heavy and fatty food. This means you should avoid oily foods. Abstain from snacks as well as cold, heavy and rich meals. Do not include sweet, sour and salty foods in your diet. Give preference instead to warm food and drinks. Eat spicy and astringent food. Meals should be light and dry.

Foods suitable for the Kapha-type are:

Eggs: scrambled egg

Meat: prawns, poultry, game

Vegetables: nearly every type of vegetable – aubergines, lettuce leaves, cauliflower, Broccoli, chicory, fennel, green beans, green leaf vegetables, potatoes, garlic, car-

rots, okra, peppers, parsley, mushrooms, radishes, Brussels sprouts, beetroot, red cabbage, asparagus, bean sprouts, celery, white cabbage, onions

Grains: buckwheat, barley, maize, millet, some white rice (basmati rice)

Pulses: all pulses with the exception of white and black beans, as well as Soya products

Herbs, spices: all spices apart from salt.

Particularly suitable are turmeric (curcuma), ginger, cardamom, coriander, cloves, black pepper, cinnamon

Dairy products: buttermilk, low-fat milk, ghee (a little), full-cream milk

Nuts, seeds: pumpkin seeds, sunflower seeds

Fruit: apples, pears, dates, figs, guavas, pomegranates, cranberries, dried fruit

Oils, fats: ghee, safflower oil, corn oil,

almond oil, sunflower oil (all in small quantities)

Sweeteners: honey

The following are not recommended for the Kapha-type:

Meat: lamb, beef and pork, seafood

Vegetables: cucumbers, pumpkin, sweet potatoes, tomatoes, courgettes

Grains: brown rice, oats, white rice or wheat (in large quantities)

Spices: salt

Pulses: Soya products, white and black beans

Dairy products: sour milk, ghee, yoghurt, cheese, quark, cream, full-cream milk

Nuts, seeds: all nuts

Fruit: avocados, bananas, sweet melons, sweet grapes

Sweeteners: molasses, syrup, sugar

THE EFFECT OF THE RASAS AND THEIR QUALITIES ON THE THREE DOSHAS

In Ayurveda, the rule is to eat a balanced diet. This means that, if possible, all six rasas (see page 53ff.) are unified in a meal and one makes sure, when preparing food, that the six flavours (see page 55) are given consideration. The flavours and characteristics effect each dosha differently. Through suitable foods you can balance and permanently stabilise Vata, Pitta and Kapha.

The rasas and their characteristics effect the three doshas as follows:

Vata
These rasas are stimulating: spicy, bitter and astringent as well as the characteristics of lightness, dryness and coldness. The following flavours have a calming effect: sweetness, sourness and saltiness, as well as the characteristics of heaviness, oiliness and hotness.

Pitta
Spiciness, sourness and saltiness are flavours that have a stimulating effect, as well as the characteristics of hotness, lightness and oiliness.
The sweet, bitter and astringent rasas are calming as well as the characteristics of coldness, heaviness and dryness.

Kapha
Sweet, sour and salty are stimulating, as well as the characteristics of heaviness, oiliness and coldness.
Calming flavours are spicy, bitter and astringent, as well as the characteristics of lightness, dryness and hotness.

APPENDIX

GLOSSARY

Abhyanga
"Loving hands"; relaxing and calming whole body massage, which is carried out by two Ayurveda-therapists at the same time

Agni
Fire; one of the ➤ mahabhutas. The Ayurvedic teachings describe agni as playing a role in the area of digestion and metabolism, among other things.

Ahara
Diet

Ama
undigested food

Asanas
Different yoga positions

Bheda
The last stage of ➤ kriyakala

Brahma
Creator of the universe in Hindu mythology and therefore the original founder of Ayurveda.

Dhatus
The seven body tissues

Dinacharya
Daily rhythm

Doshas
The three energies of life in the human body: Vata, Pitta, Kapha

Gandhusa
Mouthwash with sesame seed oil for strengthening the gums and resistance to disease-causing agents.

Ghee
Clarified butter; melted, dehydrated butter

Gunas
The three fundamental qualities of the mind; ➤ ragas, ➤ sattva, ➤ tamas

Kapha
One of the three doshas (water and earth)

Karma
"Deed"; a destiny which is determined by good as well as bad deeds in the present life and effecting future reincarnations

Kriyakala
characterises the six phases in the development of an illness

Mahabhutas
The five eternal elements; ether or space, air, fire, water and earth

Malas
Waste products; the most important are stools, urine and sweat

Mutra
Urine; one of the malas

Panchakarma
A five-part purification therapy

Pitta
One of the three doshas (fire)

Pizzichil
"Royal therapy"; whole-body oil massage, combined with a heat treatment

Pranayama
"Mastering breathing"; respiratory exercises in yoga

Purisha
faeces; one of the ➤ malas

Rajas
Activity; one of the three ➤ gunas

Rasas
The six flavours: sweet, salty, sour, spicy, bitter and astringent

Ritucharya
The seasonal rhythm

Sattva
Inner peace; one of the three ➤ gunas

Surya Namaskara
"Sun Salute"; a yoga exercise in twelve parts

Sweda
Sweat; one of the three ➤ malas

Swedana
Sweat therapy

Tamas
Passiveness; one of the three ➤ gunas

Three-doshas
The three energies of life in the human body: Vata, Pitta, Kapha

Vata
One of the doshas (space and air)

Veda
The four holy books of knowledge in Hinduism

PRONUNCIATION OF THE SANSKRIT WORDS

Sanskrit is the name of the old Indian standard language. It means "completed" or "put together". It is common practice to pronounce the words using the phonetics of English.

INDEX

INDEX